The
POWER
of PRAYER

The POWER of PRAYER

INSPIRATIONAL STORIES OF DIVINE INTERVENTION

LYNN VALENTINE

PREMIUM PRESS AMERICA
NASHVILLE, TENNESSEE

THE POWER OF PRAYER by Lynn Valentine

Published by PREMIUM PRESS AMERICA

Copyright © 2002 by Lynn Valentine

ISBN 1-887654-73-9

Library of Congress Catalog Card Number: 2002091253

PREMIUM PRESS AMERICA gift books are available at special discounts for premiums, sales promotions, fund-raising, or educational use. For details contact the Publisher at P.O. Box 159015, Nashville, TN 37215, or phone toll free (800) 891-7323 or (615)256-8484, or fax us at (615)256-8624.

For more information visit our web site at *www.premiumpressamerica.com.*

Cover and Interior Design by Bob Bubnis/BookSetters

Cover photo by David Wyatt Schnitzer

First Edition 2002
1 2 3 4 5 6 7 8 9 10

CONTENTS

DEDICATION

To you, my heavenly Father—for showing me the way. For holding my hand in church that morning. For leading me when I was lost. Loving me through one of the most difficult times in my life. For listening and for teaching me personally, the power of prayer.

THEN YOU WILL CALL UPON ME AND GO AND PRAY TO ME,
AND I WILL LISTEN TO YOU.
AND YOU WILL SEEK ME AND FIND ME,
WHEN YOU SEARCH FOR ME
WITH ALL YOUR HEART.
—JEREMIAH 29:12–13 NIV

THE GREATEST PRAYER ANYONE CAN PRAY IS,
"THY WILL BE DONE."   —LEHMAN STRAUSS

ACKNOWLEDGMENTS

My thanks and hugs go out to all of the wonderful people who have so generously shared their stories with us. I have learned much from you about faith.

To George and Bette—Thank you for believing in an idea and turning it into a reality.

To my children who are an answer to prayer—and my proof that unconditional love exists.

And finally, to my husband Bob. I am so completely filled with joy, and love, and awe, at the wonderful journey the God we serve is taking us on together.

—Lynn Valentine

LORD, HELP ME TO REMEMBER
THAT NOTHING IS GOING TO HAPPEN TO ME
THAT YOU AND I CANNOT HANDLE TOGETHER.

INTRODUCTION

Life is sometimes like a storm. At times, it comes at us with such force that all we can do is get down low on our knees and pray for it to pass. While it rages, we can hear the sound of its power as it uproots and scatters what is around us and we wonder why the voice that stilled the storm way back when remains silent.

Usually, only from the perspective of time, can we look back on the storms of life and realize that sometimes God will still the storms, and sometimes He is in the storm with us, weathering it out until it ends.

This book does not try to explain God. It doesn't attempt to show why God moves or doesn't seem to move when we pray. It does give an account, however, of those who fervently prayed and saw God do something great. It tells of others who thought God wasn't listening to them, but found out later, that He had another plan in mind. There are yet other stories of many who have weathered the storms of life, found a way to tilt their wings of faith to catch the air, and let it lift them to a higher place, above the storm, and closer to Him.

I pray that this book helps you do that.

Sincerely,
Lynn Valentine

JOE

Joe is my nephew. One day, we got a call saying he was in an accident—a terrible accident that the doctors said he wouldn't live through.

Joe's cousins, Zach and Casey were in town visiting. All young guys in their late teens, they liked having a good time and knew where to find it. They planned to join Joe's friend Ryan, and go to a baseball game; but, when plans fell through, they did the next best thing and played baseball instead. After that, it was off for pizza, and then a little offroading in a monster truck that his cousin's stepdad owned. It was a great day to be young.

Darkness had long since taken over the sky, so it wasn't easy to see the how the terrain fell. But that was part of the fun. Zach and

Casey would take the first ride, while Ryan and Joe would follow in Ryan's Honda CRX.

After about 15 minutes of driving crazy and having a blast, Zach just about lost control of the vehicle and went up on two wheels. Luckily, the truck landed back on all four tires without damage, making for a spectacular show and probably giving the next riders a stunt they would need to top.

Next, it was time for Joe and Ryan to get behind the wheel. They hopped in and raced on the dark dirt roads that night at about 50 miles per hour. They were having the time of their lives until the tires caught some soft dirt and the truck suddenly lost control.

It skid until it hit another dip in the road that caused the truck to flip. It rolled and tumbled, over and over again.

As it rolled, the passenger side where Joe was sitting was crushed, knocking him out cold. Then his seatbelt ripped, tossing him inside the cab a few times before throwing him through the window.

Joe was thrown in the path of the tumbling truck. It rolled over him, crushing him, tearing open his stomach, rupturing his spleen, and fracturing his skull.

After the truck crushed him, the tire found his leg, grabbed him and then slung him 60 feet away from where the truck finally wound up.

When the truck came to a stop, Ryan climbed out of the vehicle and searched for Joe. In the darkness, no one could see where he was, but he listened for the moaning sounds and eventually found his way to Joe's side.

Zach and Casey were too far behind the truck to have seen the accident; but once they reached the top of the hill, and saw the aftermath of it all, they began to panic.

Ryan then ran to his car and drove to a pay phone to call an ambulance while Zach cradled Joe in his arms. He tried to cover the wounds—to stop the bleeding from Joe's leg, but his fingers slipped through the torn skin to the exposed bone.

"Don't you die on me Joe," he said desperately, "don't you do it."

Once the ambulance showed up, they quickly transported Joe to Riverside Regional Medical Clinic. On the way to the hospital, one medic asked another if they had gotten ID on *the body* yet. Joe could hear them talking and felt it as the medic was searching for his wallet.

"Is this kid Joe White?" one medic asked.

"Yeah it is. Why? Do you know him, Rick?"

"Yeah, this kid is my next door neighbor."

Rick Cannady, Joe's next door neighbor, was now Joe's life support. Three times on the way to the hospital Joe flatlined; but each time, he was brought back.

Once Joe was in the emergency room, the immediate opinion from all the doctors was that Joe was not going to make it through the night. The doctors began talking to my family about unplugging him and donating his organs. All except one doctor. Dr. Borovi. She got to work, sewing, mending setting and fixing. His spleen was removed and the hole in his stomach was closed using skin grafts from his shin.

Joe remained in a coma for four days; and during this time, papers were brought for his mother to sign for donating his organs.

Meanwhile, prayer went out. Calls were made to relatives, relatives called friends and prayer chains grew to form a hedge around Joe.

One prayer warrior in particular, June, was more familiar with this kind of situation than most. Her son Danny had been in an accident as well. He, too, was not supposed to live. Even if he were to make it, she was warned that he would be in a vegetative state.

June prayed though and watched as God put her son back together again. The boy that would be bedridden and dependent for the rest of his life went on to make the dean's list in college and was recognized as being in the top percentage of college students nationwide. She knew better than anyone that it wasn't the doctors that had the last word.

In the meantime, Joe's doctor kept fighting for him t0o. Despite a problem with insurance, she wouldn't let go and never gave up. Neither did the prayer warriors. June would get up often in the middle of the night and beg God for His mercy for this boy that she never even met.

Joe's mom prayed for God to give him back in any condition.

Joe's aunts, uncles, grandparents, sisters and cousins begged for healing as the prayer chain grew.

God answers all prayers. Sometimes He says no, but this time, He said "yes".

Joe woke up.

After 12 days in intensive care, Joe was transferred to a rehabilitation hospital to learn how to walk, talk, eat and do just about everything else he needed to know how to do. A blank slate had to be rewritten as his life was rebuilt. He was alive.

Today, Joe is a little bit happy-go-lucky. He doesn't seem to look at the world the same way as the rest of us do. Having fun, enjoying each moment that comes his way, is pretty much his priority in life. The things that bother most of us–like bills, co-workers, traffic, and cars that don't run right–just don't seem to phase him.

Maybe I should be a little more like that. Maybe we all should. Maybe all of us should worry less about the things that won't even be a memory a few weeks from now and celebrate life as if it could be gone tomorrow—as the gift from God that it truly is.

—Lynn Valentine

LISTEN TO MY CRY FOR HELP, MY KING AND MY GOD, FOR TO YOU I PRAY.
IN THE MORNING, O LORD, I LIFT MY VOICE;
IN THE MORNING I LAY MY REQUESTS BEFORE YOU
AND WAIT IN EXPECTATION.
PSALM 5:2–3

IN THE MIDST

*When it comes to prayer, the most common questions
come when a child is involved. I can't begin to explain
how and why God answers these prayers. After all, I lost
my baby sister to tragedy. And yet, her passing is what
eventually led me to find my writing ministry.
This is the story of a girl who fell from a high place, but
was lifted up to an even higher place in prayer.*

We were ready to build our dream home. To save money, we got together with three other couples, bought around a hundred acres and set out to do as much of the work as we could possibly do on our own.

Our family was a great team: Eric, my husband would vacuum as Cory, my 11-year-old, and my 4-year-old daughter, Ericka, would sweep and pick up scraps. I thought this house would be filled with memories of how we came together to build something beautiful. One evening though, a very different kind of memory was made.

As usual, we got to work cleaning up after the builders had left. This time we worked on the second floor with Eric running the vacuum as Ericka swept and I picked up scrapwood from the balcony. The vacuum was loud—nearly deafening as it echoed through the unfinished wooden halls and rooms of our house.

Finally, Eric finished. When he turned off the powervac, the racket gave way to an equally intense quiet. My hearing was so acute I could have heard a pin drop. That is when I heard this odd sound like a broom handle hitting the concrete foundation below.

Ericka had been sweeping.

I looked around, she was gone. Fear gripped me as I rushed to the end of the balcony to see Ericka. . . lying unconscious on the floor below! Screaming, I flew down the stairs. By the time I got to the ground floor, Eric was already at her side, having vaulted over the balcony to get to our baby.

We tried to wake her for the longest time. Finally, her eyes blinked open, rolling upward and to the left—a sign of head trauma.

Unable to speak, I took Ericka into my arms as Eric ran to get the car. We were in such a secluded area, we felt that it would be faster to take her to the hospital than to have an ambulance make the trip all the way there and back.

The Power of Prayer

We flew toward the hospital and tried to call for help on the cell phone, hoping for an escort, but nobody could find us. In the meantime, Eric tried to talk to Ericka, asking her questions, trying to keep her awake. She'd recite her name, and answer "yes, ma'am" or "no sir" to the questions he'd ask as she cried.

I cried too.

At one point, she asked Eric to sing "Jesus Loves Me". With a shaky voice, he sang, but finally broke down before the end.

Ericka finished it for him.

After what seemed like forever, we arrived. As hospital staff took over her care, she began to throw up. Immediately they began IVs, X-rays, CT scans, etc., to determine the extent of the damage to the right side of her head. During her tests, we saw blood coming from Ericka's right nostril.

As the medical team worked, we thought back to the accident to figure out what happened. We concluded she was pushing the push broom and backed off the edge in between the studs of the wall which were twelve inches apart. She must have fallen through the ceiling.

We contacted family and friends to begin a prayer chain.

The prayer chain grew, eventually making it to my cousin Eydie in Louisiana. As soon as she heard what had happened, Eydie felt an immediate and intense pain on the right side of her head. She began praying for Ericka with her husband.

As soon as they spoke the word "amen", Eydie's pain went away and she knew right then that Ericka would be fine.

Meanwhile, back at the hospital, minutes crawled like hours until finally the doctor came in to see us. To our amazement, he said Ericka only had a minor concussion! Praise God, we were overjoyed! A nurse commented to me "You know, children are so resilient." That is true, but it was God that made this miracle happen.

Soon after, she was released from the hospital. We praised the Lord for His blessings and for the many who had interceded in prayer for Ericka.

A year later, something wonderful happened. I had taken Cory and Ericka to a new photographer in our area. She is a believer, with a deep love for the Lord. Inside our pack of pictures, she left this note:

"I'm trying really hard to see through teary eyes to reply to this. You won't believe this but here goes: A year ago, I was sitting in my office where I used to work when a friend came in. He started telling me that he wanted me to pray about something. I said "Sure, what is it?" He started telling me about a precious little girl named Ericka who had just fallen 12 feet to a concrete slab and had been rushed to the hospital with head injuries. I immediately started praying and alerted our entire prayer group by e-mail to ask them to pray also. I never dreamed that one day I would actually get to see this little miracle, much less get to take her picture. This is totally amazing to me. Our God really is an awesome God!"

— *Kristi Griffin*

MY LITTLE DAUGHTER LIETH AT THE POINT OF DEATH: I PRAY THEE,
COME AND LAY THY HANDS ON HER, THAT SHE MAY BE HEALED;
AND SHE SHALL LIVE.
—MARK 5:23 NKJV

I AM GOING OUT ON YOUR PATH LORD. I PRAY
YOU WOULD GO BEFORE ME, BEHIND ME, AND
BE IN MY FOOTSTEPS.   —GAELIC PRAYER

LIVING PROOF

*Sometimes the answers to prayer are hard to see, and
sometimes they are so obvious that just thinking of them
can bring believers to their knees.
This is one such story.*

It was raining so hard that we could barely see. Things were fine when my husband (Ray), and I loaded up our six children and headed out to Frankford. But on our way home, the drizzle became a rain that became a downpour.

Ray was doing his best to drive; but eventually, even the kids were begging him to pull over. I had never seen it rain this hard—visibility was zero, even with the windshield wipers going at top speed.

Unable to continue, Ray pulled over to what he thought was the side of the road.

Behind us came the headlights of a transfer-truck, barreling full speed down the road. Just then, the wind gusted a brief view of where we were. We realized in horror that we had pulled over on a narrow, two lane bridge. We were not even pulled all the way over!

With no time to get out of the way, Ray shouted for the kids to close their eyes and pray. He looked at me and said, "We're gonna die."

The truck lights came up brighter by the milli-second. Now on top of us, we all closed our eyes and braced for impact.

Nothing.

Another gust of wind and the truck was gone.

God loves us. We are living proof of that.

—Darlene Zumwalt

WITHHOLD NOT THOU THY TENDER MERCIES FROM ME, O LORD:
LET THY LOVINGKINDNESS AND THY TRUTH
CONTINUALLY PRESERVE ME.
PSALM 40:11

PSALM 37

This is the story of how bad it can get when you are just starting your family. What makes this story a little extra interesting is the contributor is the famous song writer, Dallas Frazier, who wrote "Alley Oop", "There Goes My Everything", and "Elvira". Still though, Dallas would much rather be known as a Christian than a musician. Here is his story.

My wife, Sharon, and I were living with our new born baby, Melody, in a small rental house in McFarland, California. We were just 22 at the time, with our whole lives ahead of us. But in the spring of 1962, we were going through some hard times.

I was unemployed, our old Chevy was broken down, and, to make matters even worse, I became extremely ill. We didn't have the money to go see the doctor so I suffered through it. I'll never be sure, but I think it was pneumonia.

For several weeks, I was down. I had a fever that caused delusions and my lungs were full of congestion. I was so bad off that I went from 155 pounds to 128.

We were financially strapped before the illness, and, by the time I recovered, we were at the end of our rope. Our cupboards were bare, we were behind on our rent, and, with our car broken down, I didn't even have a way to go out and find work. Then, as if things were not bad enough, an officer showed up to inform us that we were going to be evicted!

About six months earlier, in the fall of 1961, I had experienced a glorious conversion to the Christian faith. Jesus truly became the focus and purpose of my life. His word had become precious to me and by His grace I was learning to put my trust in His eternal, unchanging promises.

I remember kneeling and crying out to God for His help. I remember quoting to Him His own word—Psalm 37:25;

I HAVE BEEN YOUNG, AND NOW AM OLD; YET HAVE I NOT SEEN THE RIGHTEOUS FORSAKEN, NOR HIS SEED BEGGING BREAD. KJV

I clung to that promise as if my life depended on it! I told the Lord that I would take any job that He provided.... I said, "Lord, You know that I'm not lazy. I am willing to do anything! Lord, my car's broke down, I can't even go look for a job. Help us, Jesus!"

A day or two later, I heard a knock at our door. It was Albert Wasson, who owned a grocery store across from the high school. I attended Mc Farland High for four years and knew Mr. Wasson fairly well. A lot of the school kids traded with him and he was a respected man in the community. He was also a Christian who knew how to listen when God had something to say.

"Dallas," he said, "what are you doing these days?"

"Not very much... I sure could use a job."

"Why don't you come down to the store and work for me?"

I could hardly believe it. God had sent Mr. Wasson to my front door with a job offer! God answered my prayer!

The store was only a couple of blocks from our house, and I could walk to work, so that solved the broken down car problem. Mr. Wasson was a kind and thoughtful man to work for and he even gave me a 10% discount on my groceries. Praise the Lord, there was no eviction and there was food on the table. God *does* answer prayer—sometimes in very unexpected ways!

The Power of Prayer

In 1987, I bought a personalized license plate that reads: PSALM 37. I still have it. Once in a while, someone will make mention of the tag, and it gives me a beautiful green light to testify of the Lord's miraculous, merciful power. And I share with them the story I have just shared with you.

—Pastor Dallas Frazier

Once I was young, and now I am old. Yet I have never seen the godly forsaken, nor seen their children begging for bread.
Psalm 37:25 NLV

UNTO THE LEAST
OF THESE

Sometimes we experience the power of prayer when we pray and sometimes we experience it by being the answer to a prayer. This is a story of a man who listened.

My wife surprised me with a trip to New Orleans for our last anniversary. After almost 20 years of marriage, and a rough year or two, she wanted to let me know that she still loved me. Knowing how much I love Creole and Cajun food, blues and jazz, she thought New Orleans would be the perfect place to take me. Being Christians, she scheduled it all after Mardi Gras, when the crowds would be gone, and we'd have the city to ourselves.

Every meal, we ate something new. In the streets, blues players played for spare change, jazz bands played ragtime, magicians did tricks, artists did portraits, dancers danced and puppeteers performed their shows. We went into art galleries to see the work of some of the city's greatest artists and held hands like teenagers on our first date going from shop to shop from sunrise to sunset.

We really lived it up. In one day, we spent enough on meals to cover a week's worth of groceries for our whole family, but we wanted to make it a vacation we'd never forget and we did.

Finally, on the last day, hours before our plane was to take us home, we stopped at a cafe and ordered lunch. While normally I ordered things that you could only get in New Orleans—cajun dishes with oysters, shrimp and crawfish—this time I had an uncontrollable urge to order a hamburger. *A hamburger with fries!*

It seemed odd. After all, I could get a hamburger anywhere and here I was, wasting my last meal in the Big Easy on a burger!

I was really surprised at myself.

When it arrived, I was amazed to see this giant hamburger on my plate that could have fed two people. It was even cut into two halves to make it easier to handle. It was so big that after the first half I was completely full. What was weird, though, was that I had this feeling like the rest of it wasn't even mine. I felt the whole time like I was eating off of someone else's plate. It didn't make any sense. Finally, when the waiter came, I asked for a to-go box.

"We're getting on a plane soon, are you sure you want to be carrying that around?" my wife asked.

"I'm giving this to a homeless person," I replied.

"Silly boy, nobody's gonna want your leftovers," she grinned.

"I have to. It's not mine. It belongs to somebody else."

Careful not to touch it too much, I packed it in the styrofoam container as my wife watched me suspiciously with that *are you feeling alright* look.

We left the restaurant, hamburger in tow, and began to walk the streets again when suddenly, a blond girl very close to my daughter's age came up to me.

"Sir, may I have your food?" she asked.

Amazed, I looked at my wife and saw that she shared the same shocked look as I.

"Sure, it is yours. It belongs to you!"

She smiled and took it with a polite "thank you" and vanished into the crowd. We tried to find her, wanting to give her some money, too, but she was gone.

Later my wife wondered aloud if maybe we had just seen an answer to prayer—if somewhere her mom or dad was praying that somebody would feed their little girl today—praying that someone would keep her from doing something terrible in order to eat.

She smiled at me, thankful that I had listened when God told me that this hamburger belonged to someone else.

—Rob Valentine

THEN THE KING WILL SAY TO THOSE ON THE RIGHT
'COME, YOU WHO ARE BLESSED BY MY FATHER, INHERIT THE KINGDOM
PREPARED FOR YOU FROM THE FOUNDATION OF THE WORLD.

FOR I WAS HUNGRY, AND YOU FED ME.

MATTHEW 25:34-35 NLT

TRADING SORROWS

It's funny how often I've seen it happen. One person
prays and God sets in motion the answer in others.
Sometimes, God is one step ahead of us though and
answers our prayers before they are spoken.

Mary had suffered from terrible, chronic pain, and, as a result, depression. For all the years I had been the worship leader at our church, I had been praying for her healing, but nothing seemed to help. At times she seemed to get better; but inevitably, she would find herself suffering again.

One day, she called me on the phone, a little more cheerful sounding than usual. It wasn't about her health though, not exactly. It was about a song.

"Bob," she said happily, "I hate to bother you, but I heard this great song and wanted to see if you could do it one of these Sundays."

"Sure, Mary," I said, always glad to get suggestions from anyone in the congregation. "What's it called?"

"I don't know," she replied, "but in it, they sing about trading your sorrows and pain for the joy of the Lord. As I heard it, it really ministered to me, and it sounded like a song our worship team could really do well."

I had to sit down and sat there in dumb silence.

"Bob..." she asked, "are you still there?"

"Yes, Mary," I answered. "You're never going to believe this, but our worship team learned that song a few days ago. It is already on the list for *this* Sunday's service."

She got choked up and so did I. You might call it a coincidence that out of the thousands of worship songs out there, she would call me about the very song I just learned, but Mary and I know better.

—*Rob Valentine*

THE LORD IS MY STRENGTH AND SONG, AND IS BECOME MY SALVATION.
—PSALM 118:14

SET IN STONE

This story comes from a man of God.
He is an air-conditioning contractor by trade, but his
main purpose in life is serving the Lord.
One of his favorite sayings comes from St. Francis of
Assisi, who said, "Preach the Gospel at all times.
If necessary, use words."

Friday morning I got a call from the Mayor's brother, Mr. Durham. He needed me to send a service man over to his new house to turn on his new heating and cooling unit for him. He was eager to move in as they just had the electricity turned on and had a new driveway poured.

My serviceman arrived unaware of the fact that the concrete was still wet. He drove down the driveway leaving tire tracks in his wake, not realizing what he had done until he got out and his own feet sank into the cement.

That afternoon, Mr. Durham called to inform me that he had two, half-inch deep tire tracks running down his driveway. He had called his concrete man who examined the damage and told him that all he could do was saw the drive where the tracks ended, jackhammer the damaged section out and pour it again. This would need to be done at my expense and cost thousands of dollars.

I hung up the phone, enraged at the serviceman. As I was venting my anger, a minister friend of mine named Charles Green, who happened to be in my place of business, encouraged me to come into the office to talk.

"You know," he said as the door shut behind us, "you are going to have to forgive this man."

I knew he was right, and began to calm down.

We prayed together, and I chose to forgive this man for his mistake, and added, "Lord, You will have to handle the concrete."

Monday came and I waited for Mr. Durham to call.

Nothing.

Tuesday morning came; but still, no call from Mr. Durham.

Around noon my serviceman called in on his two-way radio. He was driving by Mr. Durham's house and couldn't believe his eyes.

"A miracle has occurred!" he said, unable to contain himself. "The concrete is picture perfect! Nothing is wrong with it!"

When I asked the Lord to take care of the concrete, I was just hoping for peace of mind and that things would go well with the insurance company and Mr. Durham. I had no idea that God would simply fix the concrete.

I knew then that if I had not forgiven, I would not have been blessed in this way. As a young Christian, ignorant of a mighty God and His ways, I began to study forgiveness and realized that nearly all of what afflicts us has it's roots in bitterness.

Since this has come up, whenever I pray for anyone over any problem, I usually ask if there is any unforgiveness in their hearts that we can pray about first. After that curse we put on ourselves is lifted, then God can get to work, smoothing out the deepest gouges in our hearts before they are set in stone.

—*Ken Carpenter*

AND WHEN YE STAND PRAYING, FORGIVE, IF YE HAVE OUGHT
AGAINST ANY: THAT YOUR FATHER ALSO WHICH IS IN HEAVEN
MAY FORGIVE YOU YOUR TRESPASSES.
MARK 11:25

HOW DO I KNOW THAT GOD CARES ENOUGH
TO LISTEN TO MY PRAYERS?
BECAUSE HE IS MY FATHER.

JUST ASK

This is a light-hearted story,
about a kind-hearted God.

A few years ago, our family was going through some very hard financial struggles. We always had faith and believed that God would provide and He always did.

On one particular occasion, I was out in the backyard with my three little children. It was a hot, sunny day, and we were just enjoying the beauty of it all when I thought to myself, *it sure would be nice to have a popsicle for all of us right now.*

We didn't have any in the freezer and didn't have the money to go buy any. So, I thought, *God wants to give us the desires of our hearts, and no prayer is too small for Him so why not just ask?*

So, I prayed with a grin on my face, asking the Lord to please send us a popsicle.

I know, you're thinking to yourself, "Who would ask for something like that?" Well, I did.

The next thing I know, I heard the doorbell ringing. I went through the house to find a milkman standing at the door. He asked if I knew about their services and products. I told him that I didn't. So, he handed me a product guide and said that if I'd like to order, he would be back next week to pick it up. Then, as he turned to leave, he said "Oh, by the way, here are some product samples." He reached into a thermal pouch and handed me four assorted frozen treats!

There was no way that this man knew that I had three little ones in the back yard. Yet he handed me the exact amount needed for each of us! So, in conclusion, let me say, God is your heavenly Father, so don't be afraid to ask for a treat now and then.

—Jeri Nasci

THIS IS THE CONFIDENCE WE HAVE IN APPROACHING GOD:
THAT IF WE ASK ANYTHING ACCORDING TO HIS WILL,
HE HEARS US.
1 JOHN 5:18

Shadow of the Cross

This is one of those great stories that friends like to send over the internet. I thought it beautiful how God can use the testimony of prayerful believers and the image of that cross on Calvary to save the lost, just in time.

A young man who had been raised as an atheist was training to be an Olympic diver. The only religious influence in his life came from his outspoken Christian friend.

The young diver never really paid much attention to his friend's sermons, but he heard them often. Every time they spoke, it seemed like he would slip God in there somewhere. Even when he didn't speak of God, Jesus, and all, he seemed to still be preaching. The diver liked him though, and tolerated his proselytizing as it was good for a lively debate.

Truth be told, as time went on, something inside of the diver wanted to believe badly enough to keep on listening. He wanted to hear more about this Jesus who loved so much that He let Himself be hung on the cross for His friends.

One night the diver went to the indoor pool at the college he attended. The lights were all off; but, as the pool had big skylights and the moon was bright, there was plenty of light to practice by.

He was preoccupied with thoughts of eternity, wondering if there was a God or not. The words of his friend echoed in his mind in the silence of the night. As he climbed to the highest diving board he asked "How do I know that you love me God?"

As he turned his back to the pool on the edge of the board and extended his arms out, he saw his shadow on the wall.

The shadow of his body was in the shape of a giant cross.

There was the image of Jesus, magnified by the lights. The arms that could have summoned legions of angels to destroy the crucifiers, were stretched out, instead, waiting for the nails that would save all of mankind.

Instead of diving, he knelt down and asked God to come into his life.

As the young man stood, the main flood lights came on, nearly blinding him. A maintenance man had walked in and turned the lights on.

The young man looked below to see that the pool had been drained for repairs.

He had been saved twice this night.

—Anonymous

GREATER LOVE HAS NO MAN THAN THIS,
THAT A MAN LAY DOWN HIS LIFE FOR HIS FRIENDS.
YOU ARE MY FRIENDS...
—JESUS
JOHN 15:13–14

LIFE IS THE CHILDHOOD OF OUR

IMMORTALITY.   —GOETHE

THE COLOR
YELLOW

Alex is a colorful friend of mine who works at our local grocery store. He never fails to put a smile on my face, and has this way of making everyone feel important. He is a wise man of God, who openly shares His faith in this story of answered prayer.

Last year I participated in the Wednesday night Bible study on "Dreams". The class revolved around dreams and visions in the Bible, our dreams and visions in modern times, and, how God can speak to us through our dreams.

I was raised in Hungary. As a boy, I witnessed horrific scenes of the Jewish people being persecuted and killed during this time. The

47

Jews wore a yellow Star of David on their clothing and were killed because of this. After witnessing these terrible events, I could not even bear to look at the color yellow, as every time I saw it, I was reminded of what I had seen these poor Jewish people suffer. Even at night, I had terrible nightmares about it.

In the class, I began to pray to God to reveal things in my dreams to me. The class taught us that God can heal through our dreams. I was not thinking about this memory of the color yellow at the time, and wasn't praying specifically to be rid of this curse, but God new my pain before I did.

That night, I had a dream.

In it, I stood in the midst of a field of yellow flowers. Rows and rows of them, millions of them, going as far as the eye could see. Fields and fields of them, with proud yellow petals stretching up, drinking in the sun.

Were these flowers each standing for a person who had fallen? Was this God's way of saying that for everyone who proudly wore yellow for Him, he would take care of forever?

I woke up feeling very relieved and peaceful about the color yellow and knew that God had sent me a message. On the way to work that morning I noticed all the yellow flowers blooming. Not long afterward,

I had to wear a yellow uniform at work and actually liked it. I knew God had sent me a message and had helped me to heal from this terrible memory.

Suddenly, after one dream, yellow was not the color of the persecuted, but rather the color of celebration. Yellow was the most beautiful color in the world.

—Alex Kiss

HEAL ME, O LORD, AND I SHALL BE HEALED;
SAVE ME, AND I SHALL BE SAVED:
FOR THOU ART MY PRAISE.
JEREMIAH 17:14

JESUS IS GOD SPELLING HIMSELF OUT, IN A LANGUAGE MAN CAN UNDERSTAND.

—S. D. GORDON

HOW DO YOU SPELL MIGHTY?

This story was sent to me by a friend. It tells of how sometimes when we don't see the answers to our prayers, others can.

Last Wednesday night at our church service, Pastor Ted read a letter from an elementary school teacher that attends East Hill Church. The gist of the letter was as follows:

Last school year my third grade classroom was made up of boys and girls that seemed to be poster children for tragedy. Each child came from dysfunctional families, many were undernourished and uncared for. Some lived in abusive homes and were either beaten, bruised or battered by other members of their family.

My heart ached for these kids, so, before the next school year began, my husband and I decided to come into the classroom and pray over each desk in the room. We prayed that God would place an angel behind each and every child throughout the coming year to watch over them and protect them.

A month or so after the year had started, I gave the kids an assignment to write about what they would like to be when they grew up. Everybody was busy wrestling with their dreams, searching their minds for what they thought best suited them, when Andrew raised his hand.

"How do you spell 'mighty'?" he asked.

I spelled it for him and, as he scribbled the word on his paper, I asked why he needed that word.

He looked up at me and replied, "When I grow up, I wanna be a 'mighty man of God'."

The boy next to him gave him a curious look and said, "What's that?"

Unable to say anything, I watched as Andrew told the boy what he had learned in Sunday school. "It's a man who puts on the armor of God and is a soldier for God."

Tearfully, I began to walk away, thankful that this boy was already what he had wanted to be, a mighty man of God. Before I got too far though, he motioned for me to come back and bend down. In a whisper he said, "Do you believe in angels?"

"Yes," I said with a smile.

"Can people see them?" he asked.

"I think so, sometimes," I answered.

"Good," he said, "because I see an angel standing behind each kid in this room...."

—*Anonymous*

WATCH OUT THAT YOU DON'T MISTREAT ONE OF THESE LITTLE ONES. REALIZE THAT THEIR PERSONAL ANGELS ARE CONSTANTLY IN TOUCH WITH MY FATHER IN HEAVEN.
—MATTHEW 18:10

OUR LIVES ARE A REFLECTION, OF WHAT WE THINK ABOUT GOD.

—ANONYMOUS

REVIVAL

*Our worship leader told this story at church one Sunday
morning about how God answers prayer
in His timing.*

In Charlotte, North Carolina, a farmer invited some Christian friends to come to his house to pray. It was the early 1930's and there was great revival spreading through the land which was called "The Great Awakening". The farmer was concerned about this and felt a burden to pray.

Sometimes, it is out of our own need that we pray; but for people who pray as a way of life, sometimes they feel an urge, a prompting if you will, deep inside, that causes them to pray. This is the way it was for the farmer.

THE POWER OF PRAYER

As his friends gathered at the house, they prayed long and hard for God to raise up a man from their city at this revival—a man who would carry the gospel to the four corners of the world.

When the prayers ended, the farmer no doubt watched to see who God would choose to carry the Word to the world. But the revival ended with no immediate answer to prayer.

The farmer was happy though to see his teenage boy converted at that Crusade.

His son's name was Billy Graham.

—Anonymous

THEREFORE, GO AND MAKE DISCIPLES OF ALL THE NATIONS,
BAPTIZING THEM IN THE NAME OF THE FATHER AND THE SON
AND THE HOLY SPIRIT. TEACH THESE NEW DISCIPLES TO OBEY
ALL THE COMMANDS I HAVE GIVEN YOU.
AND BE SURE OF THIS:
I AM WITH YOU ALWAYS, EVEN TO THE END OF THE AGE."

MATTHEW 28:18–20 NLT

I ONCE WAS LOST

I must confess that I am more than a little fascinated with angels. The whole idea of God sending His angels to intervene in our lives is amazing. One verse in the Bible which is quoted at the end of this story makes me wonder—how often have I spoken to an angel?

At seventeen, life can look like it is full of promise or it can seem empty and hopeless—all in the same day. It is a scary time when happy and sad seem to walk hand in hand down an uncertain and treacherous road. Being part child and part adult, you learn that some decisions are forever and that life isn't as forgiving as it used to be when mistakes are made.

For me, it seemed like the blank pages in my diary were leading up to a tragedy. I was miserable at home. I was messing up in school, getting bad grades, hanging out with kids I really shouldn't have been with—whom I didn't even like. We didn't go to church in our house so I didn't really have good influences around me. I had just broken up with my boyfriend at the time and my best friend said she was moving away to another state. It just all seemed to be too much to handle, so I decided to run away.

I left home after school. I was so scared that my mom and dad would be mad; but no matter how badly I wanted to turn around and go home, I just couldn't. I walked for the longest time.

I knew and believed in God. So I sat down and prayed.

All of a sudden I felt a soft hand on my shoulder. I looked up to see a kind looking lady wearing a funny little hat. There was a warmth in her hand that passed through me and seemed to instantly make me feel better.

She sat down, apparently in no hurry to get anywhere, and gave me her complete attention. She seemed to know what I was going through and exactly what to say to comfort me. We talked for over an hour.

I stopped crying and began to smile when I heard a horn honk and I looked over my shoulder. It was Mom and Dad. They had been out looking for me and wanted me to come back home. I smiled so big at them and waved. I stood up and turned back to thank the sweet lady that had kept me company, but she was suddenly gone. I couldn't see her anywhere. She vanished, without even a goodbye. Confused, I shrugged my shoulders and walked to the car.

Mom and Dad told me of how they drove around looking for me and they were so happy that I was all right.

I told them about the sweet lady who was sitting with me on the bench that helped me see that life's wasn't so bad after all.

"What lady, honey?" Mom asked. "We saw no lady there."

I insisted I was talking to her the entire time and told them of how she made me see that everything was going to be okay if only I'd go back home.

Mom just said she was glad I had my guardian angel with me that day. I am, too. Thank you God for taking care of me.

—Leslie Small

DON'T FORGET TO SHOW HOSPITALITY TO STRANGERS, FOR SOME WHO HAVE DONE THIS HAVE ENTERTAINED ANGELS WITHOUT REALIZING IT!
HEBREWS 13:2

GOD ASKS NO MAN WHETHER HE WILL
ACCEPT LIFE.
THAT IS NOT THE CHOICE.
YOU MUST ACCEPT IT.
THE ONLY CHOICE IS HOW.

—HENRY WARD BEECHER

IT IS WELL WITH MY SOUL

We are caught between a kind God, and an unkind world. When tragedy comes sometimes our faith flounders as we blame God for the actions of people. It is easy to love God and to praise Him during the good times, but what if we could learn to praise Him even when all is lost...

Horatio Spafford was a prominent lawyer and investor with a wife and four beautiful daughters. Life couldn't have been better for him as he had all that a person could want. He had wealth, power, a kind heart and he was also a Christian who counted Ira Sankey and Dwight Moody among his friends.

He did not keep his money to himself either. When the great Chicago fire of 1871 raged through the city, killing 300 and leaving 100,000 homeless, he was in their midst, bringing his resources to bear to help feed, clothe and house those who were displaced by the fire. However, the fire took its toll on Horatio, too. Many of the businesses he invested in were consumed by the blaze, and he, too, was hurting. Still, he spent over two years working to help others.

Finally, exhausted by his work, his doctor suggested he take a vacation. He decided to follow Ira and Dwight to one of their crusades and then go on to Europe. He booked passage on the *S.S. Ville Du Havre* in November of 1873.

Unexpected business caused Horatio to stay behind; but, rather than let his work spoil his family's vacation, he sent them along with the promise he would meet them on the other side of the ocean as soon as possible.

On November 22, just off of Newfoundland, the *Lochearn* collided with *Ville Du Havre*. Within a few minutes, the ship went down. From Horatio's family, only his wife survived. When she arrived in Wales, she sent a message to her husband:

SAVED ALONE.

THE POWER OF PRAYER

A broken-hearted Horatio set sail to meet his wife. Having lost so much, he prayed to his God for the strength to continue and to see this through.

At one point in the voyage, the captain sent for him. On the bridge he told Horatio that they were in the place where the ship went down that took his daughters Maggie, Tanetta, Annie, and Bessie from him.

He looked out over the water, and then got out some paper and a pen and wrote what would one day become one of the most beloved songs in the church;

When peace like a river attendeth my way,
When sorrows like sea-billows roll,
Whatever my lot, Thou hast taught me to say
It is well, it is well with my soul.

My sin—oh the bliss of this glorious thought!
My sin—not in part but the whole,
Is nailed to the cross and I bear it no more;
Praise the Lord, praise the Lord, oh my soul.

And, Lord, haste the day when my faith shall be sight,
The clouds be rolled back as a scroll,
The trump shall resound,
And the Lord shall descend
Even so—it is well with my soul.

In the midst of his great sorrow, after losing four daughters to terrible tragedy, his faith was so strong that instead of blaming God, he claimed God's promise that someday, all would be right—that when the trials that we face are finally at an end, no eye would be stained with tears.

In the very place where his children died, a song of praise was born that would bless generations to come and God was glorified.

—*Lynn Valentine*

WHEN I SAID, "MY FOOT IS SLIPPING,"
YOUR LOVE SUPPORTED ME.
WHEN ANXIETY WAS GREAT WITHIN ME,
YOUR CONSOLATION BROUGHT JOY TO MY SOUL.
PSALM 93:18–19 NIV

THY WILL BE DONE

Too often we say "THY will be done," but mean, "MY will be done." This is the story of a man that knew how to pray for His healing.

In December 1999, my husband was in his woodworking shop in our basement, building a toy box for my boss' grandson. With Christmas just days away, he had a lot to do.

As he was just downstairs, I could hear him working and didn't pay much attention when he was running his tools. But on this day, I heard him call out my name, followed by the sound of wood hitting the concrete floor.

I answered, but he remained silent. Now running, I got to the basement door and flung it open to find him standing there with a towel wrapped around his hand. Immediately he told me that I needed to drive him to the hospital.

Assuming that he had cut fingers off on his table saw, I rushed him to an emergency room that was 20 minutes from our house. He was in extreme pain. As we drove, he explained to me that as he was cutting a board on his table saw, the board kicked back and caught the middle finger on his right hand. He said that it was cut pretty badly at the knuckle. He also told me that he knew the finger was broken because he could not straighten it at all.

After arriving at the emergency room, I saw his finger. The gash over his knuckle was so bad that you could actually see the bone. The finger was definitely broken. X-rays indicated that he had severed the tendon that controlled all the movement for this finger.

A surgeon was called in and a screw and a pin had to be placed in the finger. He wore a cast, all the way up to his elbow for two weeks. When it came off, he had no use of his right hand. I had to cut up his food and do anything for him that required both hands. It was sad to see someone who was once so skillful with his hands depending on others for the simplest of chores.

Then, one day, I overheard him talking to our son. He seemed to be crying. When I came in to find out what was wrong, he held out his right hand to me and said, "How hard do you want me to squeeze?"

After giving me a squeeze, he told me that he found himself laying awake in bed at about 5:26 A.M. He decided to pray and asked God to fix his hand.

"I prayed 'Lord, if you want me to have the full use of my hand again, that would be great! If not though, then I will understand.'"

"After that," he recounted, "I put my hand up in the air and actually felt someone grab it."

We went to see the therapist, who measured the strength of his hands. They were amazed. He then told her the story. She sent for a colleague to come look and he retold the story of the answered prayer.

The second therapist grabbed my husband's right hand and holding it replied "I must touch the hand that has touched the nail scarred hand!"

—*Marcia Maners*

AND HE SAID UNTO ME, MY GRACE IS SUFFICIENT FOR THEE: FOR MY STRENGTH IS MADE PERFECT IN WEAKNESS. MOST GLADLY THEREFORE WILL I RATHER GLORY IN MY INFIRMITIES, THAT THE POWER OF CHRIST MAY REST UPON ME.
2 CORINTHIANS 12:9

INSTEAD OF TRYING TO PERSUADE GOD TO
BEND THE STRAIGHT LINE OF HIS WILL,
TO HARMONIZE WITH US,
WE SHOULD PRESS OUR POOR CROOKED
SELVES TO THE STRAIGHT LINE OF HIS WILL
TO FIND HARMONY WITH HIM.

—EDWARD LEIGH PELL

PERSONAL
RECOMMENDATION

This is one of the greatest prayer stories I have ever heard. This is the story of a man who called out to God and watched as God not only answered the prayer, but actually took care of the problem personally.

had a great job in sales, and was doing okay for a guy my age. I still had some dues to pay, but if everything kept going the way it looked like it would go, my future would be set. With a young wife, a baby on the way, I had all the motivation I needed to do well and set out to make them proud.

Then, one day, my boss (let's call him Mr. H) asked me to do something unethical. It wasn't just a little unethical either. It was all the way unethical. So I left, never to come back again.

Now with a baby on the way, and no recommendation from my last job, I had to find work. While I was on my way up in sales, it had been my first sales job in my field. Without the recommendation, I had to go backward for the first guy who would give me a chance.

One thing led to another and, eventually, I wound up finding an estimating job 2 hours away from home, resulting in a 4 hour a day commute. I hated it. The people were fine, the job wasn't so bad; but where I was moving up the ladder, now I was in a go-nowhere situation making less money. I hated the job and I hated the guy who forced me to work there—Mr. H.

Every day as I sat in traffic, my hate for him grew. As I took estimates on the phone, I would draw very detailed cartoons on my desk calendar of him getting beat up, blown up, hit by a train... you name it. My boss must have thought I was in need of psychiatric help.

With every bad turn by life took, I blamed Mr. H. for causing it. My anger consumed nearly every waking moment. I am normally known for being a nice guy, but this man had made me a hateful and bitter person. My wife didn't know who I was. My son was born to a father that wasn't there for him, (as I left the house at 5:00 a.m. and didn't get home until 8:00 p.m.), and my oldest daughter was growing up without her fathers's help—all because of Mr. H.

To make matters worse, we really couldn't move closer to work. I worked in a terrible area, but we lived in a nice town, close to my wife's grandparents. So I just planned to keep looking for work in my field closer to home instead, telling myself it wouldn't be long until I found something better.

Two and a half years went by, with my hatred growing every day.

Hate is a funny thing. It can become a part of you. It's something that may start out small; but eventually, it spreads into every aspect of your life. I've heard it said that unforgiveness is the curse a person places on himself. I was cursed to be sure.

The drive was getting harder to make. The stress was becoming unbearable and then my car broke down in the worst part of town. I limped to a mechanic and found out that the repairs would clean us out. I gave him the go ahead, went outside to wait and crumbled on the curb. My hate grew as I blamed even this on Mr. H.

If I only could have kept my old job, I'd be in a Mercedes by now. I wouldn't have missed so much of my kid's growing up, I wouldn't be broke right now...

To underscore my brokenness, hours later, when they finished my car, I got about an hour away and it stopped running again.

When I got home finally, I was beside myself. This had gone as far as it could go. I was finished with it all. I had run out of options.

I climbed to the roof of our house and prayed.

I went up there, I guess, so I could be as close to God as I could get. I wanted to beg Him to end this, to have mercy on me and help me find happiness again. I cried with that out of breath cry, for him to save me.

Nothing.

I waited for Him to say something, or do something, but there was no sign. No word.

Still though, I felt better about things.

My wife and I started going to church again. I got my Bible out again and began bringing it to work. Instead of listening to my heavy metal rock station, I began listening to Christian radio.

Days went by. Still no answer from God, but I was feeling better. It was like it was springtime inside of me. Winter was ending.

One day, on the radio, a pastor was talking about unforgiveness. I was a captive audience, with a long commute ahead of me, so I listened.

He said that unforgiveness was a curse we place on ourselves and that we can't expect God to bless us and forgive us if we aren't willing to bless and forgive others. ("For if you forgive those who sin against you, your heavenly Father will forgive you. But if you refuse to forgive others, your Father will not forgive your sins."—Matthew 6:14) He said that hate is a fire you light in your own home in hopes it will spread to your enemies house; but, in the end, it leaves all you love scorched.

As he spoke, I thought of Mr. H. Hating him was almost a lifestyle. Every moment that my mind wasn't on something, it was on revenge.

That's when it occurred to me that forgiveness is the best revenge.

Right then, I prayed. I asked God to forgive my unforgiveness. I forgave Mr. H., too, and asked that God would erase every sin that this man ever committed against me from whatever record God might keep of sin. I asked God to forgive all Mr. H. had done to me and my family so that, when he stood before God someday, no trespass against me would be held against him.

In an instant, it was like the weight of the world slipped off my shoulders. I honestly felt lighter, and what was the beginning of spring in my heart, burst into the full blown glory of summer. People began to like me more and even commented on the change.

In faith, without another job lined up, I went to my boss and told him that I needed to find work closer to home. He offered more money, but I told him that I couldn't take it. I told him that I knew I would be hard to replace and thought the only fair thing to do was let him know I was looking for another job so I could train someone else.

Here is where things really get unbelievably miraculous.

I usually checked the paper on Sundays for jobs. Weeks went by, without anything coming up in the classifieds. Then one Saturday, at a convenience store, I had an overpowering urge to pick up the paper. I never bought the Saturday paper. It seemed like a waste when all the jobs were listed on Sunday; but, like a magnet to steel, I was being pulled.

When I got home, I opened it and my eye went directly to an ad which read;

Wanted: Christian company seeks Product Manager

It then went on to completely list all of my qualifications. I was so closely matched to this job that it was more like reading my own resume than an ad.

Looking up at my wife, I said, "I found my job, honey."

I answered the ad and went in for the interview. After a couple of meetings, they offered me the position.

The president of the company later told me that I got the job because I got a great recommendation from someone high up.

God.

Here, as Paul Harvey would say, is the rest of the story.

They had decided on someone for my position; but, at the last minute, gathered in the boardroom and prayed that if God had someone better for the job, He would bring that person to them.

They decided to run the ad on an off-day—a Saturday—for only one day and asked God to have the right person answer the ad.

Although the ad was run in a highly competitive job market, I was the only one who responded.

I realized then, that it was hate and unforgiveness that kept God from blessing me. Once I let it go, the floodgates opened and I got a job that was infinitely greater than the one I had to give up, working in ministry.

For two and a half years, I thought God had abandoned me; but in fact, He was waiting all along for me to find my way back. Once I did, He not only set me up with a better job, but He even gave His personal recommendation.

—Name withheld on request

Now turn from your sins and to God,
so you can be cleansed of your sins.
Then wonderful times of refreshment will come
from the presence of the Lord, and He will send Jesus,
your Messiah, to you again.
Acts 3:19

HE WHO SPREADS THE SAILS OF PRAYER WILL
EVENTUALLY FLY THE FLAG OF PRAISE.

—ANONYMOUS

BECOMING GOD'S
ANSWER TO PRAYER

This is another prayer story that I heard at church. It shows how fine tuned God's planning can be when it comes to having His will be done.

Tony was invited to speak at a Christian college chapel service near where he lived. When he arrived, he went into the chapel and was greeted by several men who led him to a back room where they wanted to pray for him. They prayed that the service would go well and that those who listened would learn more about God.

As they prayed, however, one guy didn't seem be on the same program as everyone else. Instead of praying for the service like the rest of the guys were, he was praying, and praying hard, for this friend of his—a guy named Charlie.

"Lord, you know Charlie... he's getting ready to leave his wife and children tonight. He told me this morning that he was going to do it. They've really been through a lot together Lord and they are really under lots of pressure. Do something God, please. You need to step in there and do something to keep this from happening. Charlie needs you Lord."

The prayer went on and on for several minutes; and as the time crawled slowly by, the man got deeper into the details, even going as far as pointing out where the guy lived. "Lord," he pleaded, "you know Charlie. He lives in that silver trailer down that road on the right side."

At this point, Tony was wondering when this was going to end. *Come on buddy,* he was thinking, *knock it off already! This is God you're talking to here. I think He knows Charlie's address!*

But the prayer kept praying. He kept going over the details, repeating himself many times about Charlie's problems, as if he wanted to make sure God remembered everything. He kept bringing up the location of the trailer and how much these people needed immediate help.

Eventually, there was an "amen" which mercifully ended the long prayer, allowing the Pastor to speak to the waiting group.

That night, after the service had ended, Tony was driving home when he spotted a hitchhiker walking along the road. He pulled over and offered the man a ride.

Tony introduced himself and the hitchhiker did likewise.

"Hi, my name is Charlie."

Tony felt his heart race, *Could it be?..,* he wondered.

"Charlie... you are leaving your wife and kids, right?"

Charlie's eyes got big, as Tony took the next exit to turn his car back around.

"Right..." Charlie said, getting concerned at what, for him, must have been a very strange moment.

Tony was coming out of his skin with excitement as he drove to where he knew the silver trailer was. *The driving directions were for me!*

"How did you know I lived here?" Charlie said, complete dumfounded.

"God told me," Tony replied, remembering back to the prayer.

When they pulled up, Charlie's wife came to the door, "You're back! You're back!" she shouted.

Charlie met her and then whispered in her ear. Her eyes got wide as he recounted details of this strange situation.

Tony went up to the porch and said, "I'm going to talk and you are going to listen." Complete with the details that he had learned earlier through the fervent prayers of another, Tony led the couple to become Christians and they began the journey that would restore their marriage.

Today, Charlie is a preacher himself and this story remains a powerful example of the power of prayer.

—Anonymous

Confess your faults one to another, and pray one for another, that ye may be healed. The effectual fervent prayer of a righteous man availeth much.

James 5:16

PRAY ABOUT
EVERYTHING

*As we pray, we sometimes ask with our head for what
we don't believe in our hearts. Faith that God answers
all prayers is important, but we have to be prepared for
the times He answers with a "no". In this story we read
about a woman who believed; and with faith,
waited for God's answer.*

Our three girls were in the 5th, 7th and 9th grades when my husband and I bought a small farm and moved to the country. We were all so excited! Now we could have animals! The girls had been taking horseback riding lessons and, instead of boarding their horses, we could have them live with us at home.

THE POWER OF PRAYER

We bought some goats and some polled hereford cattle along with one Charolais steer that had BIG horns. I have always loved and cared for animals, but this steer proved to be very ornery.

All animals have personalities. Some are very meek, some are contrary, but this steer was mean and angry! He began to show just how tough he was, too, by walking along and tearing long holes in our wire fencing.

On another day, he proved his character when he came after the girls. He chased them to the barn and up the stairs where they had to wait just out of reach until he decided to leave them alone. They were so scared!

That was the final straw! That was it... he had to leave. I was so done with him, in fact, that I suggested we pen him up, grain feed him and put him in our freezer!

My husband agreed. I called the meat packer the next day and agreed to bring him in, in a few weeks.

We didn't have a pen, but we did have a breezeway through the barn with a small fenced in area—a perfect place for the steer to stay and be grain fed for a while. We didn't have a corral with a head catcher built yet, so I parked the horse trailer in front of the breezeway to block escape. I left the door open, hoping he would get used to seeing it and get comfortable enough to go inside it.

He didn't.

I put "sweet feed" in the trailer to entice him, but he wouldn't go in. Everyday I went down to the barn to feed him grain, but he still would not go into the trailer.

Finally, the day came for our appointment with the meat packer. It was Wednesday and everything was arranged, except, of course, the steer wasn't doing his part yet. He wouldn't go into the trailer.

My husband and I devised a plan to get him to cooperate. We got up early and went down to the barn. We decided to hold the edge of a wire gate and walk behind the steer to kind of prod him along. At first, it worked great; but, as we neared the trailer, he turned around, stuck the long horns through the gate, and began pushing, barely missing me in the process!

My husband hollered, "Drop the gate—let him go—we're no match for him!" We backed off as the 1005 pound steer finished off the gate.

Deciding that this was just too much work to do on an empty stomach, we went in to make some breakfast. As I cooked, I prayed. I told the Lord that the steer wasn't worth one of us getting hurt over. After all, I could buy my meat at the grocery store. I was also feeling badly that I wouldn't be able to keep my appointment with the meat packer. I had given my word we would be there.

This just wasn't going well at all.

My husband went to get more sweet feed as I cleaned up after breakfast. As I washed the dishes, I kept praying. Finally, with my work done, I decided to walk down to the barn alone.

I said to the Lord, "*I can't* put this steer in the trailer Lord, but *you can!* I'll stand on the side of the trailer where I can reach the door and, after you put him in, I will close it."

I stepped up to the side of the trailer. The steer was down the breezeway cautiously looking at me, and me at him, when my husband, who had just come back form the co-op, hollered to me, saying, "He's never going to go into the trailer with you standing right there! He can see you!"

"I can't help it!" I called back, "I told the Lord I would stand here and shut the door after *He* puts the steer in the trailer."

I turned to face the steer again, my mind still praying, *Please, Lord,* You *put him in.*

All at once, he came. His head was actually lifted up some, like someone had a ring in his nose and was pulling on it! He didn't hesitate, but walked right up and into the trailer.

I hurried to shut the door awestruck at the way God answered my prayer. I hollered and danced around, praising the Lord.

When we went to church that night, I got up and testified to the most gracious, marvelous God we serve. He cares about everything! Let's pray about everything!

—Sharon Frazier

BE CAREFUL FOR NOTHING; BUT IN EVERY THING BY PRAYER
AND SUPPLICATION WITH THANKSGIVING LET YOUR REQUESTS BE MADE
KNOWN UNTO GOD.
AND THE PEACE OF GOD, WHICH PASSETH ALL UNDERSTANDING, SHALL
KEEP YOUR HEARTS AND MINDS THROUGH CHRIST JESUS.
PHILIPPIANS 4:6–7

MOST PEOPLE DON'T GO TO GOD TO FALL IN
WITH HIS WISHES AND PLANS;
MOST GO TO PERSUADE HIM TO FALL IN WITH
THEIR WISHES AND PLANS.

—EDWARD LEIGH PELL

AFTER AMEN

I've heard it said that the reason we have two ears, but only one tongue, is because we should listen twice as much as we speak. If this applies to prayer, then we should listen intently for the still, small voice of God...

We decided to go to my Dad's farm for New Year's Day and spend the weekend. It really is lovely out there, with fishing ponds, horses and plenty of beautiful scenery to relax in.

Everyone went, including my brother, husband, my 2½-year-old son and a family friend—Jack. We had to coax Jack to go with us, but I really felt that he needed the break as bad as we did.

A couple of days before, however, I had a very bad dream. I pay attention to my dreams, as they have warned me of impending danger before. Waking up, I knew that something was about to happen to someone close to me.

I didn't know who was in trouble, or what the danger was that might be waiting for them; but I cried and prayed just the same, asking God with all my heart to protect all the members of my family.

When we arrived at the farm, we all decided we wanted to do different things. I wanted to go fishing. My brother and husband decided they would check the ponds and my son wanted to ride one of the horses. In the meantime, my father was listening to music and relaxing in the cottage.

While I was fishing, Jack was fixing the saddle of the horse my son was riding since it wasn't done properly.

Some time went by as I got lost in thought, watching a can of soda floating nearby. I felt all my tensions melting away into nature.

Suddenly, though, I heard a voice say, "Stop what you are doing and come here!".

I didn't think twice. I left the fishing pole and started walking around the lake to where the voice came from. As I did this, I saw my son's small body was floating in the water. I threw myself in and got hold of him, pulling him to shore as sharp sticks and twigs ripped at the clothes I was wearing. I screamed for help at the top of my lungs. My son wasn't breathing and his color was almost purple.

Jack came running to us and began working on my son, giving him artificial respiration and CPR. The weird thing is that he had never done it before and learned it in high school in Peru many, many years ago. I thought back to how I had to convince him to come, and realized now, why I felt so strongly about his being there.

As everyone made it to the scene, my son started to get his color back and cough up the water. We didn't know how long he had been under, but he was on his side now, coughing all the water up and I was thanking God for bringing him back to me.

Beginning with a dream that warned me of danger, and then the voice that called me to drop what I was doing, I feel God was answering my prayer personally.

—Angela

HE SHOWED YOU THESE THINGS SO YOU WOULD REALIZE THAT THE LORD IS GOD AND THAT THERE IS NO OTHER GOD. HE LET YOU HEAR HIS VOICE FROM HEAVEN SO HE COULD INSTRUCT YOU.
DEUTERONOMY 5:35–36 NLT

LIFE IS A DREAM,

DEATH IS THE AWAKENING. —BEAUMELLE

THE TOUCH

In the 23rd Psalm, the Psalmist writes:
"Yea, though I walk through the valley of the shadow
of death, I will fear no evil: for thou art with me..."
*This doesn't say that God will always walk us around
these valleys, or over them. It says through them.
This is the story of two such trips with God.*

Five years ago, I lost my son to cancer. He was 10 when he died. Surviving this was tough for us, but we had a daughter to take care of, so we leaned on God for the strength to go on.

A few days before the anniversary of my sons passing, my daughter began to complain of a pain in her leg. Fearful that something serious was wrong, we took her to the doctor. After days of testing, we found out that she had cancer. What made things worse, was that the day we found out was on the anniversary of my sons death, five years earlier.

Words cannot explain how we felt. How we found the strength to live through the death of my son, I didn't know. Getting through this seemed impossible.

Still, I gathered my strength for my daughter.

Family and friends were very supportive. They offered to pray and I prayed, too, with all my heart. I must confess though, I was beginning to doubt that God even cared. After all, I had prayed for my son and still lost him.

One day when I was sleeping, I heard a voice that said: *Do not worry, everything is going to be all right.* I felt so much peace and truly believed it. I told my husband we do not have to worry, that everything will be all right.

My husband had a dream as well. Here is his account:

My name is Orlando, and on the night before our daughter's chemotherapy was to begin, I fell asleep and had this dream.

In my dream, I was sitting in my church with my daughter beside me. While I was praying for her, my son came around the altar with someone I couldn't recognize. My son was giggling and ran up to sit on my lap. I told him how glad I was to see him, but that I knew he would have to go back to heaven.

He just giggled and touched my daughter's leg. At that point, the other person that was with him also touched her leg.

I told my son, "Your sister has cancer on her leg. Please go ask God to help us!"

My son just kept on laughing and the other person touched my shoulder.

Just then, the telephone rang, waking me up. It was the doctor calling to tell me that my baby did not have cancer—he claimed she was misdiagnosed. I fell on my face and thanked God for this miracle.

During my praying and praising, I realized that the person with my son in the dream, who touched my daughter's leg and tapped my shoulder, was Jesus. Amen.

—*Orlando & Miriam Alices*

AND JESUS PUT FORTH HIS HAND, AND TOUCHED HIM, SAYING,
I AM WILLING; BE THOU CLEAN.
MATTHEW 8:3

I PRAY FOR THE STRENGTH TO LIVE THROUGH
WHAT I MUST LIVE WITH,
THE WILLINGNESS TO LIVE
WITHOUT WHAT YOU WITHHOLD
AND THE DESIRE FOR ONLY THE THINGS YOU
DESIRE.

MIRACLES AND FAITH

Having given birth four times, it wasn't hard for me to imagine, at least to some small degree, what it might have been like for the mom in this next story. As much as we love our kids, though, it pales in comparison to how much God loves them.

My daughter, Chelsea, was born early in the morning. She was 8 pounds 6 ounces and simply perfect in every way. I played with her little hands, ran my fingers through her hair, caressing the cheek and the chin of my beautiful baby girl. I memorized every feature, like all parents do, and made it a point to savor each moment.

I had just settled in to sleep after feeding her for the first time when the nurse came in and woke me up. She told me I needed to go to the nursery and speak with the doctor. I walked in and saw him standing there, looking in disbelief at a sick little baby. My sweet little baby was in respiratory distress and we needed to do something fast. The hospital we were at was not capable of handling the problem and I needed to choose another one immediately.

Here I had only been a mother for a few hours and already I was facing the possibility of losing her. During the next hour, as we waited for the Life Flight, all we could do was to keep watch. I cried so hard. All I wanted to do was hold her and make everything all right. All I could do was pray.

Early that morning, Life Flight arrived and they whisked her out the door. I would not be released until noon and by the time I got home it was close to 1:00 P.M. We left immediately for the other hospital. When we arrived, we were met at the NICU door by a nurse with a most serious look on her face.

"You need to come with me and speak with the doctor," she said.

All I wanted to do was to see my daughter. I remember wondering if we were too late, wondering if she was already gone. Somehow I found the ability to walk. Maybe she knew my thoughts by the expression on my face, but the nurse said quietly, "You can see your daughter in a minute, you just really need to talk to the doctor first."

The next five minutes were a blur. The doctor told me that Chelsea was declining rapidly. He put her on a ventilator; and, when that didn't help, they put her on a jet ventilator. However, it was not helping her either. Her blood pressure had bottomed out and she had fluid in her lungs. Even with hand bagging her, her oxygen levels couldn't be raised to a safe level. Her heart was not working right and neither were her lungs.

"We have two options," he said, "you can stay here and hold her till the end, or you can opt to fly her to another hospital 300 miles away from here, where they can place her on E.C.M.O."

I had never heard of the procedure before then. It was explained to me that Extra Corporeal Membrane Oxygenation is when they bypass the heart and lungs and let a machine do all the work for them. It requires surgery, massive amounts of donor blood and specially trained medical staff. It is dangerous, but everything else had been tried and failed. This was it. The decision was easy. Chelsea would go to the other hospital.

Once again, we sat by her bedside watching, waiting and praying. Dr. Bob Couser called from the other hospital and we spoke at length about what would happen upon arrival there. There were many drawbacks to this type of treatment—many of which I was not sure if I could handle. I sat quietly and cried after I spoke with him.

I thought about what this would mean for her. I imagined the pain she would endure, the possibility of brain damage and possibility of death from the E.C.M.O. Then I prayed, not only for her; but also for strength and courage. I prayed and put my trust in God to help her be all right.

I had to put her in His hands and in the hands of the doctors she would be delivered to that night.

Just before Chelsea left, we had her baptized. It was beautiful, considering where we were. They laid a handmade christening gown over her, as she was too ill to put it on. The pastor baptized her, hugged us, and then spoke so many kind words of hope.

When the helicopter landed and they rushed her to the roof, I took a picture of her. I needed something to hold until I could see her again. Then, in an instant, she was gone. It was like watching an angel take flight.

Long hours later, we arrived at the other hospital. It was after 4 A.M. due to bad weather and the long drive. Chelsea had been connected to E.C.M.O. before we arrived and was still unstable in critical condition. She lay there motionless. They gave her Pavulon, a medication to paralyze her for surgery, and this was the after effect.

The doctors and nurses were compassionate, but honest. They were doing all they could, but now it was up to her and to God. They said the best thing we could do was pray.

I prayed and then questioned myself. Would she be better off going home to God? Is that what was meant to be?

"Why? Why her? Why me?" I pleaded before breaking down into tears. I was so scared.

Then, I felt this peace come over me. I can't explain it, but I was totally calm. Sitting there I felt like I was a little girl, snuggled up on my dad's lap. I suddenly knew in my heart at that moment that nothing else would go wrong. She was going to be all right.

Chelsea recovered.

Today, Chelsea is a normal and healthy five-year-old. She carries scars on her neck and chest and mine are deep within my heart. But we wear them proudly, though, as a testament to how kind God was to us.

—*Rhanah Truman*

IN MY DISTRESS I CALLED UPON THE LORD, AND CRIED UNTO MY GOD:
HE HEARD MY VOICE OUT OF HIS TEMPLE, AND MY CRY CAME BEFORE HIM,
EVEN INTO HIS EARS.
PSALM 18:6

GOD PROMISES A SAFE LANDING,

BUT NOT A CALM PASSAGE.

—BULGARIAN PROVERB

MY FIVE ANGELS

Some never see with their eyes what God is doing around them. Occasionally, though, one of us gets a rare glimpse at glory.

One day, life is good. The next day, the peace that was taken for granted is the deepest desire of the heart. This past August, my normally healthy 19-year-old daughter was laying comatose on a respirator. She had a rare pneumonia and was not responding to any antibiotics. The doctors were stumped and didn't hold out much hope for her.

On the 14th day of this ordeal, I lay crying myself to sleep as I had for the previous 13 days. Again, I prayed to God and in the depths of my pain I cried out to God:

"Angels, I need lots and lots of angels, God! Send them around my little girl, one isn't enough!"

No sooner than I cried out, I had a vision of my daughter in her darkened I.C.U. bed. It was like this powerful image, as clear and as vivid as a dream. Circled around her were five human shapes, almost like shadows.

"I need more than five, God, please!"

I cried, but a sense of well being settled over me and I fell off to sleep.

The next morning, I hurried back to her bedside. My heart nearly leapt out of my chest with joy when I saw her, awake, and breathing on her own. Tears began running down my cheeks and I began thanking God in my heart. I knew immediately that God sent just the right amount of angels to take care of my daughter.

My joy gave way to questions on how she felt. She told me her throat hurt and then, she said something odd.

"They must've had me on some really powerful drugs because I was hallucinating while I was out."

I asked her what she was saw in her 'hallucinations'.

"Mom, I kept seeing these five people standing in a circle around my bed. I couldn't see their features, but there were five of them."

The doctors had no explanation for her sudden recovery or for the fact that her X-rays had gone from total white out of all four lobes of her lungs to perfectly clear overnight.

"You had a miracle," one of them told me.

My daughter and I already knew this though. After all, we saw the angels with our own eyes.

—Anonymous

FOR HE SHALL GIVE HIS ANGELS CHARGE OVER THEE,
TO KEEP THEE IN ALL THY WAYS.
PSALM 91:11

LORD, I CONFESS THAT I AM NOT WHAT I
OUGHT TO BE, BUT I THANK YOU, LORD,
THAT I'M NOT WHAT I USED TO BE.

—MAXIE DUNNAN

SELAH

This story may not sound all that dramatic at first, but when you let it sink in, you'll find a blessing.

I was driving to prison with my good friend Jimmy. We used to minister to the inmates there and had a great time doing it. In fact, some of the best church I have ever had was behind bars. They sing louder, "amen" stronger; and, when it comes to praying, they don't just talk to God with that ho-hum blah blah voice you hear a lot on Sundays, they cry out to the Lord from the pits of their souls.

I loved those guys.

Maybe getting past the end of their rope did it. Charles Colson and Jim Bakker both were thankful that they went to prison because that is where they say they were truly set free. I don't know. But, I must say, that one of the greatest joys of my life was going there.

Anyway, I am getting off the subject. My story is about what happened on the way to prison.

Jimmy is a great guy. He is one of those guys who lives for the Lord. Nothing happens that he doesn't go to God first about it. He thanks God when he steps out of his house, talks to him on the way to work. He has stickers and magnetic signs all over his truck, wanting to make sure that nobody passes him without thinking of Jesus.

On this particular day, we were driving together, talking about... you guessed it. God.

I had my guitar between my legs, as I was going to lead the singing that night, and was kind of cramped in his little pickup truck. I am a little claustrophobic anyway, so, gradually I began getting in a crabby mood.

"Bob, how do you know when God is talking to you?" he asked.

"Well, for me it is just something that happens inside of me. He sounds a lot like my conscience, only stronger, He never drops it when He starts on something."

I was referring to the times in life when I just felt an overpowering urge to do something for someone for no apparent reason, only to find it was someone's answer to prayer—or make something right that wasn't really all my fault.

"Well," Jimmy said, "I've been asking God to talk to me for the longest time, and you know," he paused for a moment as if wondering if he could tell me, "I think He did say a word to me just the other day."

I wasn't in the mood for this really. I wanted to think about what music I should be doing—wondering how to sequence it and thinking about what stories I might know to get the worship going. As I mentioned, I was just a little ornery that day; so, in my mind, I decided already that he was probably just talking himself into this. I am a believer and believe that God speaks to his people, but not usually in an audible tone. Jimmy, bless his heart, loved God so much, he convinced himself that God spoke.

Again, in my mind, I decided to challenge Jimmy. I thought, *if you really spoke to him God, he will say...*

At that point, I let the first word that popped into my mind become the word.

Selah. I thought.

That was weird. I was expecting a word like "duck" or "blue" to come to mind. I didn't even know what language *Selah* was.

Jimmy interrupted my thoughts.

"Anyway, I asked God to speak to me and he said... *Shelah.*"

My heart stopped.

Not exactly the same, but close enough to let me know that it wasn't Jimmy I was challenging in my mind, it was God.

Do not put the Lord your God to the test, was the scripture I immediately thought of. I was instantly ashamed at myself for thinking so little of God that he wouldn't answer Jimmy's prayer. I wondered how I could be a believer, and at the same time, be so quick to judge the faith of another.

"Jimmy," I stuttered, "I was just thinking of the same word. . . I told God that if He were really speaking to you, to give me the same word as He gave you." I told him some of what I had been thinking, and wanted him to share my excitement now at having heard from the Lord as well!

What was odd was that now Jimmy was looking at *me* skeptically, like maybe *I* was the one who was wishful thinking.

I wish I would have blurted it out before he did, so that he would know what happened and felt the full impact of the blessing. Had I been as bold as he was—had I had as much faith—if I wouldn't have let doubt trip me up, we both would have been rejoicing together.

Later, Jimmy said he looked up *Selah*, and that it is an old Hebrew word, the exact meaning of which was forgotten some 200 years after Jesus was born. What scholars do know is that it is a musical term that probably meant "the pause, and/or 'amen' between songs".

THE POWER OF PRAYER

A pause between songs.

As a music leader, I wondered if God wasn't using this whole experience to teach me a few things.

1) God will answer a prayer however He wishes.
2) Don't be so quick to judge.
3) Instead of being so focused on the songs I sing, I should be thinking more about who I am singing them to.

I hear You, Lord.

—Rob Valentine

ALL THE EARTH SHALL WORSHIP THEE, AND SHALL SING UNTO THEE;
THEY SHALL SING TO THY NAME.
SELAH.
PSALM 66:4

PRAY TO GOD AND THEN SAY, "THY WILL,
NOT MINE BE DONE."
THE BEST LESSON I LEARNED IN GOD'S SCHOOL
IS TO LET THE LORD CHOOSE FOR ME.

—DWIGHT MOODY

PRAYER CHAIN
MIRACLE

This is the story of how believers got together all over the world to come before God to pray.

y seven year old daughter, Miranda, had a bad cold. She seemed to gradually get worse and I knew as I looked at her with mother's eyes, that something was wrong.

The doctor did a chest X-ray and found a huge tumor in her lung. They did a biopsy and found it to be malignant. I couldn't believe it. My worst nightmare had come true.

To say what you go through during this time is impossible. Only one who has been there can grasp the full weight of this burden. You get angry with God, and then desperately seek Him. You wonder if this was something that you could have prevented and then wonder if it is something you can fix. You walk with pain and sorrow, that you have to hide behind a confident, happy face as you comfort those around you.

We began to prepare ourselves for the onslaught of medical treatments that would follow, looking for strength that we didn't seem to have. You know how it is. It's like carrying something, knowing you can only hold it up for another minute, but pushing yourself to hang on indefinitely beyond that.

After we found out, we began to pray. First our family, and then our friends, began to pray. Friends contacted their friends, who contacted their friends, to pray. Then prayer chains broke out on the internet, drawing in believers from everywhere who went before God asking for a healing.

Despite the prayers, on Monday morning, the day of her surgery, the doctor called and asked us come in as soon as possible. The biopsy they had taken was malignant; but, miraculously, the next one was benign!

The doctors had no explanation, but we did. We believe we had a miracle—an answer to prayer. The tumor was removed and she was out of school for about 2 weeks. She is doing just wonderfully and the doctors brought her case before a convention of pediatric oncologists.

They were shocked! She is a case study for this hospital and they will be following her for quite some time, marking her progress.

We go back every three months so they can make sure she's okay. We go before the Lord everyday because we *know* she is okay.

—*Melissa Kelso*

O LORD, I CALL TO YOU; COME QUICKLY TO ME.
HEAR MY VOICE WHEN I CALL TO YOU.
MAY MY PRAYER BE SET BEFORE YOU LIKE INCENSE;
MAY THE LIFTING OF MY HANDS BE LIKE THE EVENING SACRIFICE.
PSALM 141:1–2

FAITH MAKES THINGS POSSIBLE.
IT DOES NOT MAKE THEM EASY.

"Oh God, Help Me!"

We live in a dangerous world in which anything can happen. In this story, we see how easily a ride home can go from routine to a matter of life and death.

Soon after Howard's conversion in 1971, he was followed home one night by five young men who were drunk and high on drugs. They were looking for trouble. When my husband stopped for a red light, they bumped into him from behind and came out of their car spoiling for a fight. My husband got out of his car to check for any damage.

They had intentions of doing serious harm to him. They started pushing my husband. My husband defended himself and got into his car and took off. They followed my husband right up to the door of our house. My husband ran into the house and got our gun. My husband held the German Luger up to the leader's head and said, "If you don't leave, I'll shoot!".

The man was so intoxicated that he didn't even realize that my husband had a gun. Fortunately, his friends realized the danger and pulled their leader away. In moments, they were gone.

The next morning my husband realized that someone could have gotten hurt. Being newly saved and fearful that the gun could even be found by one of our children, he decided to take apart the gun. During this demolition exercise, he pulled the pin out with his teeth and the gun fired. He thought the gun wasn't loaded, but did not know that there was a bullet lodged in the chamber. The bullet went through his hand, through the mattress, and into the floor. The entry wound was as small as a quarter. When it came out, it was the size of a softball. He blew a hole in his hand and his index finger was hanging by skin.

He wrapped towels around his hand and had to drive to the hospital, about 45 minutes away. While he was driving he felt light headed and had to pull over. He was passing out and in shock. Howard was dying. When he put his head down on the steering wheel, he cried out loudly from the depths of his spirit, "Oh God, help me!"

At that very instant, he got all of his strength back, his light-headedness cleared and he felt good again. We hit every green light. The cars just seemed to be moved out of our way as if we had an escort clearing out path.

He walked into the emergency room and the doctor admitted him. The doctor thought they might have to amputate a finger or a hand. They were concerned about blood poisoning, also.

That same night, a younger man than my husband was admitted to the emergency room with a gunshot wound to his hand. This man went into shock and never recovered. With Howard though, they were able to reconstruct his finger and reattach the severed tendons, muscle and shattered bones. It took over 135 stitches just on the outside of his hand to close the wound. Today, Howard has use of his hand and he still has his finger.

Praise the Lord for His salvation and His healing.

—*Carolyn Madden*

Turn to me and have mercy on me,
as you do to those who love Your name.
Psalm 119:132

ALL I HAVE SEEN TEACHES ME TO TRUST THE
CREATOR FOR ALL I HAVE NOT SEEN.

—RALPH WALDO EMERSON

WHEN JESUS SAW THEIR FAITH

I love this story. Just when you think you've passed the miracle, you'll find that another is waiting right around the corner. For anyone facing hardship, this story demonstrates that, through God, anything is possible.

In an instant, everything changed. That's all it takes. All that stands between the way things were, and the way things are, is one bad decision, one miscalculation, one mistake. It is then, that, in the same way that time is divided by B.C. and A.D., our own lives are broken into two parts—before and after.

For me, this happened several years ago when I was in a motor-cycle accident. When that life-changing moment was finished with me, I was a quadriplegic. I had no use of my legs, partial use of my right hand, no feeling on my right side, a ruptured optic nerve and short-term memory loss.

It could have been worse though.

I could have been a non-believer.

As a Christian, I knew that bad things happen to us all. Even the Apostles had it rough. Being believers didn't guarantee them a first-class, trouble free, trip through life—in fact, they dealt with terrible hard-ships—being beaten, imprisoned, rejected and even killed. So, I under-stood that being a believer wasn't an insurance policy against hard times. Instead, belief, faith and trust in God was what I needed to lean on to get me *through* the hard times. Knowing God, and realizing that I belonged to Him, eventually made me want to overcome my injuries and move forward with my life.

This realization was a miracle in itself, but more miracles awaited.

Although I was confined to a wheelchair, I was able to continue through Him in my education at Salisbury State University, Hagerstown Junior College and Prince George's Community College where I was a student in general studies and paralegal studies.

THE POWER OF PRAYER

While attending Salisbury State University in 1987, I became involved in wheelchair sports and excelled in shooting. Over the next three years, God blessed me with 39 gold medals, 14 silver and 3 bronze and opportunities to compete in regional, state, national, international, world championships and the 1988 Paralympics in Seoul, South Korea. During this time God also blessed me with 19 national and world records.

Then, shortly after being blessed with an internship with the Administrative Judge of the Circuit Court, I had begun to drift away from the Lord. After all the adversity I had overcome, and after all the success I had achieved, I found myself trying to make it on my own. This took me down a road where, spiritually, I was heading for yet another terrible collision.

Having separated myself from Him, I began to fall into a deep depression; and, the further I got, the worse things got. In the end, I attempted suicide twice, lost the love of my life (so I thought), lost a business and lots of friends.

Finally, at a place long past the end of my rope, I found myself stuck at the home of some Christian friends, unable to leave because my van was broken down. During this time, I listened as they talked about the God I used to be close to—the God who got me through so much. In my heart, I felt drawn back into my heavenly Father's arms. I became so full of the Spirit that I completely surrendered unto Him. I became active in the Church again, and eager to do His will.

This was yet another miracle, in and of itself, but more awaited.

By this time, 15 years had elapsed since I had traded my motorcycle for a wheelchair. It was then that I heard about a special healing service going on at the World Harvest Church in Columbus, Ohio. I felt that I needed to be there. I hadn't heard of the Pastor, I didn't know anything about the Church; but somehow I knew a miracle was waiting for me there.

I decided to tell my friends at church that I was going and that the Lord had placed it on my heart that I was to receive a healing—just what healing I didn't know as I had several ailments. My pastor then prayed over me in faith for that healing.

The next morning, feeling was restored to my right hand.

Praising God, I told my Pastor about it. We all knew that the Lord was in the process of doing something special with me.

Upon arrival at the church, I used my cell phone to call into the church to see if there was somewhere I could go where I could freshen up after my more than 400 mile drive. Somehow, I reached their prayer line instead! During this time, as long as we were talking, we decided to go ahead and pray right then. As we prayed, a burning sensation came over my feet. I knew that the Lord was once again at work in my body. At that point, I praised Him and accepted my healing. I revealed this to the prayer partner and asked that she keep an eye out for me so that we share the joy of being a part of God's work.

During the service, I went up for prayer. During this time, I continued to feel strange sensations in my body. As I went to adjust myself in my wheelchair, one of the ushers asked if I was trying to get out of my chair. Before I knew it, I said "I'm going to jump out of this chair in thirty seconds."

I took hold of the chair's armrest and raised myself slowly to my feet and found myself standing for the first time in 15 years.

The ushers then asked if I could walk. I didn't know what would happen, but looked down in faith to see my feet stepping out. One foot, miraculously, before the other. The next thing I knew, the Lord helped me up the steps onto the stage toward the pulpit, to give praise to God.

After returning home, I called my pastor to inform him of the awesome miracles and ask that I be allowed to go before the congregation to testify of God's glory and give praise for His mighty works. I wanted to encourage others not to give up, that they might be blessed and renewed in their faith.

Prior to going into the sanctuary that morning, the Pastor and I prayed. God had reawakened my spirit, restored feeling in my hand, given me back my legs. All that remained was my blind eye. As we prayed I took off the patch, and, once again, I could see. Everything was blurry, and remains blurry, but I can see.

I spoke at my church about the healing I received, giving all praise and honor and glory to the Lord. I felt the blessing being released and poured out over the congregation. I hope that you, too, are blessed by my story, and that your Faith is being restored. That would be the most important healing of all.

—*William A. Kent*

WHEN JESUS SAW THEIR FAITH, HE SAID TO THE PARALYTIC,
"SON, YOUR SINS ARE FORGIVEN."
HE GOT UP AND WALKED OUT IN FULL VIEW OF THEM ALL.
THIS AMAZED EVERYONE AND THEY PRAISED GOD SAYING,
"WE HAVE NEVER SEEN ANYTHING LIKE THIS!"
—MARK 2:5, 12 NIV

W H Y ?

*One question that gets asked of me often is
"Where was God on September 11th?"
Here is my answer.*

hy? When the buildings came down, I was watching, along with you, unable to understand or take in the horror of that event. For days afterward, all I could do was sit in shock, staring at the television, hoping for survivors, praying that somehow, everything was going to be all right.

In time, I began to heal. Although scarred, I was able to find reasons to smile again, but my thoughts are never far away from the tragedy that changed America forever.

During this same time, my books on the subjects of angels and miracles had come out, and I was doing radio and television interviews. All along, I hoped no one would ask the question; but, inevitably, both a radio and television host couldn't help but put me on the spot.

Ms. Valentine, where was God on September 11th?

God was there, with us, ushering into heaven all those who believed in Him—all who had found their way down the narrow road.

He was there for all of those who called out His name in those last minutes.

He was there for all of us who sat helpless, feeling hopeless— wanting us all to call out His name.

And we did.

I don't know why bad things happen. I only know that because they do, I need God.

I need His comfort, His wisdom, His promise, and His will for my life. That way, if tragedy finds me, He will be the one to usher me into the place where tragedy, pain and sorrow are no more.

My books are about miraculous ways that people are rescued, healed, or, in some way, touched by God. My prayer, and the ultimate goal of this book would be that you would add your own story to this collection by choosing God.

—Lynn Valentine

AND I HEARD A LOUD VOICE FROM THE THRONE SAYING,
"NOW THE DWELLING OF GOD IS WITH MEN, AND HE WILL LIVE WITH
THEM AND BE THEIR GOD. HE WILL WIPE EVERY TEAR FROM THEIR EYES.
THERE WILL BE NO MORE DEATH OR MOURNING OR CRYING OR PAIN, FOR
THE OLD ORDER OF THINGS HAS PASSED AWAY." HE WHO WAS SEATED ON
THE THRONE SAID, "I AM MAKING EVERYTHING NEW!"

REVELATION 21:3–5

Premium gift books from PREMIUM PRESS AMERICA include:

I'LL BE DOGGONE

CATS OUT OF THE BAG

GREAT AMERICAN CIVIL WAR

GREAT AMERICAN GOLF

GREAT AMERICAN OUTDOORS

GREAT AMERICAN GUIDE TO FINE WINES

ANGELS EVERYWHERE

MIRACLES

SNOW ANGELS

THE POWER OF PRAYER

ABSOLUTELY ALABAMA

AMAZING ARKANSAS

FABULOUS FLORIDA

GORGEOUS GEORGIA

SENSATIONAL SOUTH CAROLINA

TERRIFIC TENNESSEE

TREMENDOUS TEXAS

VINTAGE VIRGINIA

TITANIC TRIVIA

BILL DANCE'S FISHING TIPS

DREAM CATCHERS

AMERICA THE BEAUTIFUL

PREMIUM PRESS AMERICA routinely updates existing titles and frequently adds new topics to its growing line of premium gift books. Books are distributed though gift and specialty shops, and bookstores nationwide. If, for any reason, books are not available in your area, please contact the local distributor listed above or contact the Publisher direct by calling 1-800-891-7323. To see our complete backlist and current books, you can visit our website at www.premiumpress.com. Thank you.

Great Reading.   Premium Gifts.